TO TONY

WITH LOVE
AND
BEST WISHES

FROM
CHARLIE - MARGARET

Especially for

From

Date

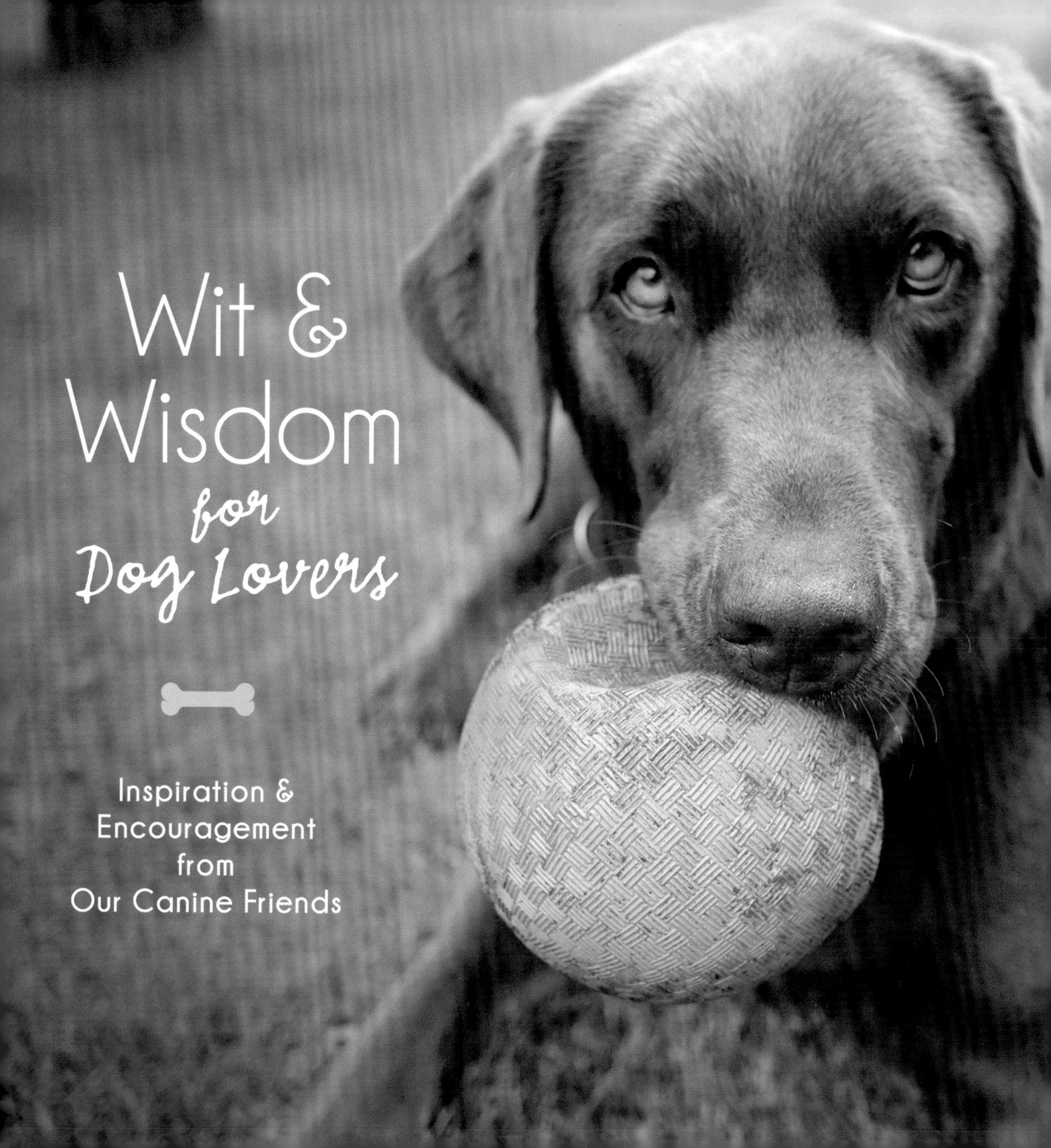

Wit & Wisdom
for
Dog Lovers

Inspiration &
Encouragement
from
Our Canine Friends

© 2015 by Barbour Publishing, Inc.

Compiled by Brigitta Nortker.

Print ISBN 978-1-63058-699-7

eBook Editions:

Adobe Digital Edition (.epub) 978-1-XXXXX-XXX-X

Kindle and MobiPocket Edition (.prc) 978-1-XXXXX-XXX-X

Scripture quotations marked KJV are taken from the King James Version of the Bible.

Scripture quotations marked NKJV are taken from the New King James Version®. Copyright © 1982 by Thomas Nelson, Inc. Used by permission. All rights reserved.

Scripture quotations marked NIV are taken from the HOLY BIBLE, NEW INTERNATIONAL VERSION®. NIV®. Copyright © 1973, 1978, 1984, 2011 by Biblica, Inc.™ Used by permission. All rights reserved worldwide.

Scripture quotations marked NLT are taken from the *Holy Bible*. New Living Translation copyright © 1996, 2004, 2007 by Tyndale House Foundation. Used by permission of Tyndale House Publishers, Inc. Carol Stream, Illinois 60188. All rights reserved.

Scripture quotations marked CEV are from the Contemporary English Version, Copyright ©1995 by American Bible Society. Used by permission.

Scripture quotations marked NCV are taken from the New Century Version of the Bible, copyright © 2005 by Thomas Nelson, Inc. Used by permission. All rights reserved.

Scripture quotations marked AMP are taken from the Amplified® Bible, © 1954, 1958, 1962, 1964, 1965, 1987 by The Lockman Foundation. Used by permission.

Scripture quotations marked MSG are from *THE MESSAGE*. Copyright © by Eugene H. Peterson 1993, 1994, 1995, 1996, 2000, 2001, 2002. Used by permission of NavPress Publishing Group.

Cover image ©

Published by Barbour Books, an imprint of Barbour Publishing, Inc., P.O. Box 719, Uhrichsville, Ohio 44683, www.barbourbooks.com

Our mission is to publish and distribute inspirational products offering exceptional value and biblical encouragement to the masses.

 Member of the Evangelical Christian Publishers Association

Printed in China.

Wit & Wisdom
for
Dog Lovers

BARBOUR BOOKS
An Imprint of Barbour Publishing, Inc.

A "Rein Check"

No human being can tame the tongue.
it is a restless evil, full of deadly poison.

JAMES 3:8 NASB

Although dogs, descendants of the gray wolf, were domesticated thousands of years ago, some still seem to have a wild side. Such was the case with Buck, the German-shepherd-mix beast we'd rescued from the pound.

Buck liked to bolt. If anyone held him (or the kitchen door) too loosely, nine times out of ten, he would break free and run for his life—usually down to the pizza parlor to pick up some fresh, just-delivered Italian rolls. One night he bolted, got struck by a car, and kept going. The next morning, my husband and I, thinking Buck had died from injuries received in the accident, broke the news about his early demise to our little girl. Ten minutes later we found Buck sitting on our porch, panting, hale and hearty, ready for his breakfast kibble.

Like Buck, the human tongue can sometimes run wild, leading us to say things we later regret. So before speaking, consider applying a "rein check" to your words, making sure they are encouraging, not hurtful. Another option may be to simply muzzle your mouth by stuffing it with a nice fresh Italian roll.

He who barks last,
barks best.

PAMELA McQUADE

A dog's bark is as much a signature as its scent.
Every bark is a full, clear statement of existence—
"I bark, therefore I am." It is unrestrained,
unedited, and unabashed.

JOHN O'HURLEY

Dogs do always bark at those they
know not, and. . .it is their nature to
accompany one another in those clamors.

SIR WALTER RALEIGH

9

Follow with Determination

The scent hound is a model of
perseverance, Lord. He holds to
a trail without deviation, all the
way to the end. May I follow
as determinedly after You
as that hound pursues the
track of some small creature.

Nothing but Love

Nothing in all creation will ever be able
to separate us from the love of God that is
revealed in Christ Jesus our Lord.

ROMANS 8:39 NLT

I was having one of those days. It began with oversleeping, which made me late for an appointment. Later, while running errands, I backed my SUV into a brand-new red Mustang convertible in a parking lot. Once home, my mood worsened, and I found myself speaking harshly to a loved one. Disgusted with myself and the day's events, I headed up to my room. There was Durham, our latest rescue hound, napping on the bed. I threw myself on top of the quilt and began to cry. The next thing I knew, the tail-wagging Durham, overjoyed to see the miserable me, was licking my face. I looked directly into his eyes and saw nothing but love.

No matter how badly our day goes or how miserable we feel, our dogs will love us unconditionally. Such is the love of God. Nothing can separate us from His all-encompassing compassion for us. Even through our tears, we have a place in God's heart. That's something to wag our tails about!

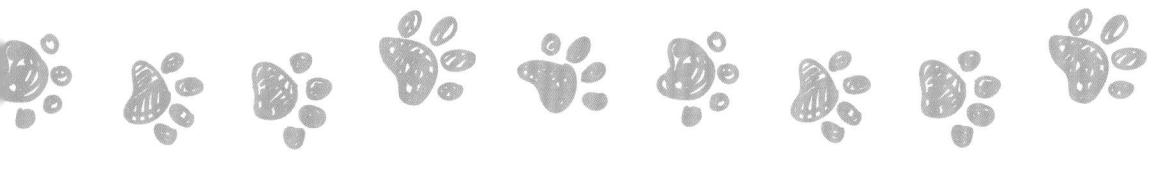

*A loving heart
is the truest wisdom.*

CHARLES DICKENS

       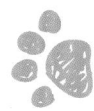 

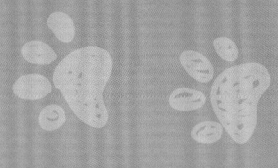

After years of having a dog, you know
him. You know the meaning of his snuffs
and grunts and barks. Every twitch of
the ears is a question or statement,
every wag of the tail is an exclamation.

ROBERT R. MCCAMMON

In times of joy, all of us wished
we possessed a tail we could wag.

W. H. AUDEN

Surely, Lord, you bless the righteous;
you surround them with your favor as with a shield.

PSALM 5:12 NIV

"The Lord lives! Blessed be my Rock!
Let God be exalted, the Rock of my salvation!"

2 SAMUEL 22:47 NKJV

You have given me your shield of victory.
Your right hand supports me; your
help has made me great.

PSALM 18:35 NLT

17

Spiritual Identity

What great love the Father has lavished on us,
that we should be called children of God!
And that is what we are!

1 JOHN 3:1 NIV

The rescue organization for which my husband and I volunteer as foster parents requires that each animal be microchipped with a unique identification number. When seven-year-old Kloey, a rat terrier, came to live with us, the rescue coordinator sent me the chip, the inserter, and a two-page explanation of the procedure. One look at the size of the insertion needle told me that it was a job for my well-seasoned vet and not for a squeamish foster parent. Kloey was going to the vet the next afternoon, so I took the chip along.

After the initial exam and vaccinations were completed, the vet tech asked if I wanted to watch the microchip procedure. I hesitantly agreed. I tried to make conversation to cover my shakes.

"I've never used the scanner," I said. "How do you do it?"

Dr. B. lifted up what looked like a very large plastic magnifying glass and ran it along Kloey's shoulders as he said, "You just do this—" He was interrupted by a single electronic beep. To our surprise, Kloey already had a chip.

Back home, as I waited on the microchip company's customer service line, a myriad of thoughts drowned out the hold music. *What was Kloey's original name? How did she wind up on the city streets so long ago? Most importantly, would she be welcomed back home?*

The music stopped abruptly, and a woman with a cheerful voice verified the chip number as one that had been assigned but never registered. My heart sank. A nonregistered chip meant that there was no address or phone number on file for the dog. My questions wouldn't be answered, and there would be no heartwarming family reunion. What a difference some identification could have made.

As our world becomes more and more populous, identity becomes ever more relevant. No one wants to say, "I'm just one of four billion. I'm nobody. Don't notice me." We spend a great deal of money and effort protecting our identity from theft. We safeguard our computer, our bank account, and our credit cards.

When it comes to our spiritual identity, we can relax. It is ensured by God Himself. In Isaiah 49:16, God says, "I have engraved you on the palms of my hands" (NIV). God promises that even foreigners who choose to please Him will be given an "everlasting name that will endure forever" (Isaiah 56:5 NIV). How much greater is the promise to those He calls His own? The New Testament states that all believers are "God's children" (Romans 8:16 NIV). Praise God for our identity in Christ.

Nobody ever saw a dog make a fair and deliberate exchange of one bone for another with another dog. . . . When an animal wants to obtain something. . .it has no other means of persuasion but to gain the favor of those whose services it requires.

ADAM SMITH

Humankind is drawn to dogs because they are so like ourselves—bumbling, affectionate, confused, easily disappointed, eager to be amused, grateful for kindness and the least attention.

PAM BROWN

A dog will look at you as if to say, "What do you want me to do for you? I'll do anything for you." Whether a dog can in fact, do anything for you if you don't have sheep (I never have) is another matter. The dog is willing.

ROY BLOUNT JR.

Every word of God is pure:
he is a shield unto them
that put their trust in him.

PROVERBS 30:5 KJV

He will cover you with his feathers,
and under his wings you can hide.
His truth will be your shield and protection.

PSALM 91:4 NCV

"But whoever listens to me will
live in safety and be at ease,
without fear of harm."

PROVERBS 1:33 NIV

23

Rest Easy

He who dwells in the secret place of the
Most High shall remain stable and fixed under
the shadow of the Almighty. . . . He will cover
you with His pinions, and under His wings
shall you trust and find refuge. . .
You shall not be afraid.

PSALM 91:1, 4–5 AMP

Our dog Durham, a Shar-Pei–yellow-Lab mixed mutt, is around
ninety pounds of pure love and muscle who spends most of his time
determined to get his daily eighteen hours of shut-eye. When the ways
of the world attempt to disturb his rigorous sleep schedule, he finds
solace in his little burgundy, green, and white afghan. This security
blanket is able to smooth Durham's hackles raised by strange dogs
walking down the sidewalk or a rapid knock on the front door.

We, too, can get our peace disturbed by the unexpected. Thank
God for providing us with His unfathomable security. In His all-
encompassing presence, wrapped in His infinite arms, we can be at
peace. With God as our covering, we need not be afraid but can rest
easy no matter what comes down our sidewalk or knocks at our door.

Dogs make us believe we can actually be as they see us.

THE MONKS OF NEW SKETE

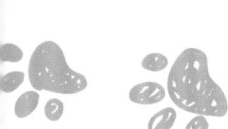 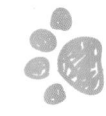    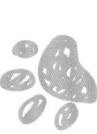 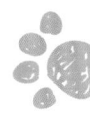 

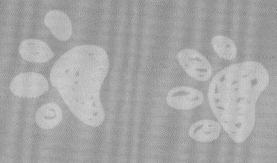

I have been studying the traits and
dispositions of the "lower animals"
(so called) and contrasting them with
the traits and dispositions of man.
I find the result humiliating to me.

MARK TWAIN

All of the animals except man know that
the principal business of life is to enjoy it.

SAMUEL BUTLER

He said: The Lord is my Rock [of escape
from Saul] and my Fortress [in the wilderness]
and my Deliverer; my God, my Rock,
in Him will I take refuge; my Shield and the
Horn of my salvation; my Stronghold and my
Refuge, my Savior—You save me from violence.
I call on the Lord, who is worthy to be praised,
and I am saved from my enemies.

2 SAMUEL 22:2-4 AMP

Be my mighty rock, the place where I can always
run for protection. Save me by your command!
You are my mighty rock and my fortress.

PSALM 71:3 CEV

A Greater Friend

A man who has friends must himself be friendly,
but there is a friend who sticks closer than a brother.

PROVERBS 18:24 NKJV

Whenever I had a problem as a child, I always found a patient and willing listener in my springer spaniel named Max. As we sat on the living room floor, Max would listen attentively while I told him about my being snubbed by a friend, getting a not-so-good grade, or getting cut from the basketball team.

Yes, dogs are definitely man's (and woman's) best friend, for not only do they have great listening skills and are always willing to lick your tears away, but most will stay by your side through field and forest. Some dogs have even been known to rescue their owners from deadly danger!

The truth is we have an even greater friend in Jesus. There is absolutely no better companion or champion in our lives than Him. Jesus, by sacrificing His own life, has already saved us from the ultimate peril—life (and death) without God. And, although dogs may come and go, Jesus, the Man who names us as His friends, will stick with us to the very end. What a friend!

*I am a much better person
with a dog in my lap.*

JOHN O'HURLEY

The great pleasure of a dog is
that you may make a fool of yourself
with him and not only will he not scold you,
but he will make a fool of himself, too.

SAMUEL BUTLER

Dogs have a way of finding the people
who need them, filling an emptiness
we don't even know we have.

THOM JONES

Best Friends

- -

Thank You, Lord, for the joys of
having a dog. Help me to find enough
time to play with him, walk him, and
care for him. May he not only be
my best friend, may I be his.

Just Perfect

"The LORD your God is with you, the Mighty Warrior
who saves. He will take great delight in you;
in his love he will no longer rebuke you,
but will rejoice over you with singing."

ZEPHANIAH 3:17 NIV

Long before we adopted our first dog, I had the itinerary of our
human-canine relationship perfectly worked out. We would take quiet
walks in the park, people in front and the dog heeling expertly on
the left. There would be obedience training (in which my dog would
surpass all expectations), and, of course, there would be games of
fetch. Lots and lots of fetch.

Two years and three dogs later, I am no longer deluding myself.
Our rat terriers love the park—for running, not walking—and absolutely
not quietly. Kloey is an inveterate barker.

Jot went to obedience training. For six weeks she hid under a
chair. In the final two weeks she emerged, but only to steal other dogs'
treats before scuttling away to eat them in private. On graduation day
the trainer was complimenting each owner on the accomplishments of
his or her dog. "Good sit," he would say, or "Way to do a down stay!"

When he got to me he thought for a moment and then said, "Well. . . she's learned that a German shepherd can't fit under that stool."

Despite a few setbacks, I never gave up. When Tilly joined our family, I got out the old tennis ball. All three dogs watched the ball bounce, roll, ricochet off the table leg, and come to a spinning stop. They yawned, stretched, and lay down for their midmorning nap. I tried again with a mint-condition rope toy, an unchewed squeaky rubber shoe, and a still-pristine ball of yarn. My dogs have perfected the art of ignoring toys.

The only game Tilly will play is hide-and-seek. One morning when we were running late for a vet appointment, I found her on the windowsill behind the draperies. She tucked up her legs to make a compact bundle, but a bit of plumy tail poked out between the blinds and gave her away. She won't willingly endure rain even when she really needs to go out. During one particularly drizzly week, I found her curled around the drainpipe below the kitchen sink. When the sun sets and she knows bedtime is approaching, Tilly will quietly slip between the upholstered flaps of the fold-out couch.

My dogs aren't what I thought they would be, but they are just perfect. Zephaniah 3:17 tells us that God feels the same way about His children. Imagine His happiness as He finds you, gently calls your name, and frees you from a tight spot. He rejoices over you. He sings joyful songs about you. In God's eyes, you are perfect. You are God's delight.

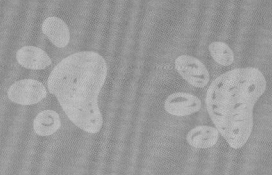

If you think dogs can't count, try putting
three dog biscuits in your pocket and
then giving Fido only two of them.

PHIL PASTORET

I care not much for a man's religion whose
dog and cat are not the better for it.

ABRAHAM LINCOLN

If a dog will not come to you after having
looked you in the face, you should go
home and examine your conscience.

WOODROW WILSON

Canine Vision

Help me, Lord, to sometimes see life through my dog's eyes. May I appreciate the joy of greeting someone I love and delight in the cool morning breeze as we take a long walk together.

Astounding Love

Love bears up under anything and everything that comes, is ever ready to believe the best of every person, its hopes are fadeless under all circumstances, and it endures everything [without weakening].

1 CORINTHIANS 13:7 AMP

Early one morning I heard Zoey barking wildly in an apparent flurry of activity. By the time I got to the front porch, I found her with a guilty, wide-eyed, pitiful face, next to my overturned, all-but-trashed, previously-beautiful, big pot of pansies.

It looked like a mouse had burrowed into the dirt and she'd had to protect the place. I could tell she was guilty. Her sheepish walk gave her away when I called her closer. Her quick obedience to "sit," then "lay," then "hush up!" was incriminating! Her long sad eyes were still filled with love for me as she lay there watching me clean up the mess, replant the flowers, and then forgive her.

A few mornings later the same thing happened, but this time two flowerpots were overturned, and I was not so forgiving. I corrected Zoey harshly, and she walked even more slowly when called. She curled up in a ball after taking her scolding and looked at me longingly, with love still in her eyes.

A few days after that, there was a third occurrence, this time on the back deck with three pots of flowers. I was livid with Zoey. Each time she clearly acted and appeared guilty. "Zoey!" I huffed, broom in hand, to clean up another pointless mess. I scolded her and angrily went about my business.

That's when my husband gently pointed out that Zoey hadn't been out all night, nor had she been out prior to him spotting the crime scene. He was right, and I felt horrible. Moreover, as I recalled each dirt-flying mess, I realized that Zoey never had any dirt on her paws or nose. Still she'd stood there, taking on the guilt, when it could not have been her at all. She probably thought she was being scolded for not catching the criminal. She'd been framed! By whom, though, was now the question.

The next night, extra lights were left on and the front door was left open, with only the locked glass door between Zoey and the unknown criminal. This sounded like a setup for a broken door. I thought about that possibility, but really, Zoey's all bark. Turned out, no broken glass and no criminal either.

The ability of a dog to love its family is always astounding. It is a great picture of how God loves me. He watches me in my fits of anger, often based on misunderstanding, and loves me still. He took on all my guilt and shame at the cross, and He always responds to me, no matter what, with longing eyes filled with love.

The dog has got more fun out of man than man has got out of the dog, for the clearly demonstrable reason that man is the more laughable of the two animals.

JAMES THURBER

The one absolute, unselfish friend that a man can have in this selfish world—the one that never deserts him, the one that never proves ungrateful or treacherous—is his dog.

GEORGE GRAHAM VEST

God will prepare everything for our perfect happiness in heaven, and if it takes my dog being there, I believe he'll be there.

BILLY GRAHAM

Your kingdom is an everlasting kingdom,
and your dominion endures through all
generations. The Lord is trustworthy in all
he promises and faithful in all he does.
The Lord upholds all who fall and lifts up all
who are bowed down. The eyes of all look to
you, and you give them their food at the
proper time. You open your hand and
satisfy the desires of every living thing.

Psalm 145:13–16 NIV

Cast your burden on the Lord,
and He shall sustain you; He shall never
permit the righteous to be moved.

Psalm 55:22 NKJV

Speak of Faith

LORD, make me dwell in safety.

PSALM 4:8 NIV

Ginger was a black Lab with a lot of personality. And talk about loyal! She would do anything for her master. When he told her to sit, she sat. When he told her to roll over, she rolled over. When he tossed the ball, she fetched it. Anything he would ask her to do, she would do. Why? Because she sensed his love.

One of Ginger's favorite pastimes was to let her master rub her tummy. She would roll over onto her back and wriggle until he noticed her. He always smiled and spoke words of love over her as this transpired. Then, as he reached down to run his hands along her belly, she would lie perfectly still, enjoying his touch. Before long, she got so relaxed she would fall asleep under his watchful eye. How wonderful it felt to know she was loved. And how she trusted him!

We have a lot to learn from Ginger, don't we? Sometimes we're so frazzled by life that we forget we have a trustworthy Master. And we're so busy that we don't draw near to spend intimate, quiet time with Him. He longs for us to curl up in His lap so that He can tell us how much He loves us. That's what being in a relationship is all about, after all. And He wants us to rest easy, knowing He's in control, even when life around us is chaotic.

It's interesting to think about Ginger's belly-up posture. Lying there on her back, she is completely vulnerable. Open. She senses no fear. Her body position speaks of faith, doesn't it? She trusts her master implicitly. In the same way, the Bible says that we can come boldly to our Daddy God, entering into His throne room, knowing we are loved. There's nothing to fear. And He longs for you to open yourself as you have never done before, sharing your deepest longings, joys, and fears. This is what real relationship is all about!

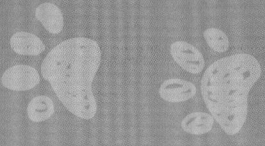

No philosophers so thoroughly
comprehend us as dogs and horses.

HERMAN MELVILLE

Isn't it amazing how powerful a dog becomes
as soon as it stretches out on the human's bed?
A fifty-pound, dead-weight dog can take up more
space than the average woman. He'll also make
her apologize for wanting more than a quarter
of the bed for her own use.

PAMELA MCQUADE

Joy will make a puppy of an old dog.

THORNTON W. BURGESS

God stays one with everyone who openly says
that Jesus is the Son of God. That's how we stay one
with God and are sure that God loves us. God is love.
If we keep on loving others, we will stay one in our
hearts with God, and he will stay one with us.

1 JOHN 4:15–16 CEV

"I will heal their waywardness and love them freely,
for my anger has turned away from them."

HOSEA 14:4 NIV

Our Stronghold

The LORD is my light and my salvation—
whom shall I fear? The LORD is the stronghold
of my life—of whom shall I be afraid?

PSALM 27:1 NIV

Durham barks as if he is fearless. Yet there are times when he is anything but.

One day my husband, Pete, brought a huge roll of bubble wrap home. He placed it in our son's room with the intention of using it as packing material to ship something the next day. Later, sitting downstairs, we heard Durham growling on the floor above. My curiosity piqued, I went to the landing, looked up at the top of the steps, and saw Durham halfway into Zach's room, his hackles raised. Alarmed, I ran upstairs and comforted a now-cowering dog. Then, not knowing what I might find, I cautiously peeked into the room. Everything looked normal except for the bubble wrap. As it turned out, that's what had freaked out our ninety-pound, muscle-bound dog!

Sometimes we, too, growl at the things we fear—then cower in fright. But God has told us He's with us through everything! With Him, we have nothing to be afraid of. We can face bubble wrap with courage, knowing that God is our stronghold.

It's a poor watchdog who
sleeps with both eyes closed.

THORNTON W. BURGESS

There is only one smartest dog in the world, and every boy has it.

UNKNOWN

Study hard, and you might grow up to be president. But let's face it: Even then, you'll never make as much money as your dog.

GEORGE H. W. BUSH

57

Two Species

Lord, You have placed this
helpless puppy in my arms.
As two very different species,
we're likely to have communication
gaps. Please help me appreciate
my dog, and nurture growth and
understanding between us.

In Translation

We do not know what we ought to pray for, but the
Spirit himself intercedes for us through wordless groans.
And he who searches our hearts knows the mind of
the Spirit, because the Spirit intercedes for God's
people in accordance with the will of God.

ROMANS 8:26-27 NIV

Durham has trouble telling us what he wants. That's because he has
the same bark when requesting his bone as he has for requesting
kibble, water, carrots, permission to get up on the couch, and access
to the outside facilities. So, whenever he barks, we have to offer each
item, one at a time, until we hit upon his actual desire.

Sometimes we, too, have trouble communicating. It can even
happen in our prayers to God. Certain situations come up in life and
we don't know how to handle them. We aren't even sure exactly how
to pray. Fortunately, God has provided us with the Holy Spirit. He can
interpret any request we have on our heart—even if we ourselves don't
know how to express it!

If only we had such an interpreter to translate our dog's barks,
groans, and whines. Where is Doctor Dolittle when we need him?

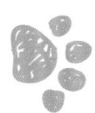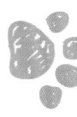

How very unlike are poodles and greyhounds! Yet they are of one species.

ADAM SEDGWICK

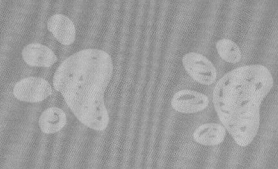

On a popular dog-intelligence-rating
scale, the bloodhound comes in well
below the "smart" rating. But ask any human
if he'd rather have the top-smarts-rated
border collie scent out his missing child,
and he'd surely prefer that "stupid"
bloodhound's top-rated nose!

Pamela McQuade

Food for Wisdom

- -

Lord, before I had a dog,
I never thought so much about
what he should eat. Now I often
think about his treats, scraps,
and dog food. Help me feed
my dog wisely and well—
but not too much.

Sink Your Teeth Deep

I will delight myself in thy statutes:
I will not forget thy word.

PSALM 119:16 KJV

Some dogs are quirkier than others. Take Bandit, for instance. Even as a puppy, this bloodhound liked to chew, and not just the usual things. Sure, he liked the occasional dog bone. And he loved a good tennis shoe. But what really got Bandit excited. . .was fabric. He loved the feel of flannel between his teeth, so no blanket in the house was safe.

After losing a couple of really nice comforters and blankets, Cindy, his owner, finally wised up. She bought a small blanket from her local supercenter, just to appease Bandit. If he was going to chew on fabric, at least it wouldn't be her expensive bedding. She prayed this would keep him preoccupied. . .and also prayed he wouldn't swallow any of the fabric!

Less than two months later, Bandit had chewed over forty baseball-sized holes in what was now affectionately called his "chew-chew blanket." Thankfully, he didn't swallow the missing pieces of fabric.

Are you a "chewer" like Bandit? Do you sometimes find yourself chewing on things you shouldn't? God never intended for us to chew on things that might hurt us. Just the opposite, in fact! If you've got to chew, at least chew on the right things. Start with the Word of God. Sink your teeth into it. Spend time meditating on it. You will find that the more time you spend chewing on good stuff—love, joy, peace, righteousness, long-suffering, etc.—the less time you will have to replay and relive old injuries. Before long, your painful memories will be just that. . .memories. And they will fade more with each passing day as you feast on the Word.

Golf seems to be an arduous way to go for
a walk. I prefer to take the dogs out.

PRINCESS ANNE

Leash: A long, weblike device that
allows a dog to control his human
and pull her in the opposite direction
of where she would otherwise go.

UNKNOWN

Whenever I hear a dog continually
barking, my reaction is one of relief—
that it's not my dog making all that racket
and inciting the neighbors to call the police.

JOHN MCCARTHY

Short Days

Thank You, Lord, for my lively
little pup. Remind me that these days
of puppyhood are short. Give me
large doses of patience and love,
along with enough determination
to train her for a lifetime.

Seizing Opportunities

See then that you walk circumspectly,
not as fools but as wise, redeeming the
time, because the days are evil.

EPHESIANS 5:15–16 NKJV

Dogs are nothing if not opportunists. Our next-door neighbors were having a Fourth of July party for their family, and their family has a lot of kids. Between our yards there is only a line of well-spaced shrubs. During the afternoon, four or five of the smaller children were sitting in a row of lawn chairs, eating sandwiches, laughing, and giggling at the games of the older children—and of some silly adults. One girl raised her arms up and back in laughter and joy. In her right hand was about a quarter of a sandwich. I had my collie Symba out in the yard, playing ball with him before I put him on the leash and took him for a walk. Seeing the girl's arm go up with the sandwich, Symba zipped like lightning between the bushes and behind the row of chairs, and in one leaping motion snatched the sandwich from the girl's hand, landed, and ate it—as cleanly as the slickest pickpocket and about fifty times quicker!

I was shocked, embarrassed, and snickering at the same time.

My wife screeched "Symba!" and started laughing then ran to the girl to make sure her hand was okay. But Symba had snatched the sandwich so cleanly that the girl didn't even notice until she pulled her hand down to take a bite. When she looked at her empty hand, her eyes got wide. But the kids around her had seen it; some gasped, some were giggling even louder. One who knew our dog yelled, "Yay, Symba!"

How skillful are you at seizing opportunities? Snatching chances? Seeing it and going for it? Not for yourself, as with Symba, but for others and for Jesus?

Jesus and His disciples ran into a funeral procession; family and friends were taking a young man to be buried. Jesus found out that the weeping mother was a widow, and the boy her only son. He immediately said inside Himself, "This won't stand!" He showed God's power and taught God's mercy by immediately raising the son and happily handing him back to his mother.

Parents brought children to Jesus to be blessed; in one moment He illustrated humility, ministry, mercy, and God's kingdom. Sometimes I'm good at opportunity seizing, and sometimes I'm not. One little opportunity I love to seize is with unexpected responses to common phrases. For example, when someone at work exclaims, "Oh my Lord!" (or something worse), I'll often reply, "Yeah, He's the One you need to talk to." Or, when they declare, "Lord, have mercy!" often I reply, "Yeah, if He doesn't, we're all cooked!"

He is an undersized lion.

A. A. MILNE

Dachshund: A half-a-dog high
and a dog-and-a-half long.

HENRY LOUIS MENCKEN

There are all sorts of cute puppy dogs,
but it doesn't stop people from
going out and buying Dobermans.

ANGUS YOUNG

Training Moment

A well-trained dog is a lifelong pleasure.
Thank You, Lord, for keeping me patient
in teaching my dog how we can share
a safe, happy, and loving life.
May I always faithfully show my
dog the best way to live.

A Banquet

I have not departed from your laws,
for you yourself have taught me.
How sweet are your words to my taste,
sweeter than honey to my mouth!

PSALM 119:102–103 NIV

Jot came into our lives two years ago. As first-time pet owners, my husband and I had many questions about the behavior of this nine-pound nine-year-old rescued rat terrier. Why did she eat grass? What compelled her to paw her bedding into a heap? The most puzzling thing of all was her attitude toward food. The vet told us not to worry. He determined that Jot had a decreased sense of smell as a normal result of aging, which accounted for her loss of interest in food.

A few days after the diagnosis, we returned from a night out to find a line of paper confetti on the floor. We followed the trail from the front entryway to the bedroom where it culminated in a mound of shredded personal documents that had been tipped from their container. Atop the makeshift haystack sat Jot, contentedly licking a discarded Slim Jim wrapper that had been at the very bottom of the pile. Since then we've had plenty of evidence that Jot's olfactory function is unimpaired. Jot doesn't lack ability, but she does need a strong motivation to act.

So do I. I know that the Bible is full of nourishment, but it takes some doing to make me eat. I'll study carefully for Sunday school—if I'm teaching it. There's no problem spending an hour probing the scriptures for a certain verse—if I want to use it in a greeting card. This habit of scriptural snacking has often kept me from being truly full of God's Word.

Psalm 119:103 describes the Word of God as being "sweeter than honey." Paul urged believers to move from spiritual milk to the more strengthening meat of the Word (see Hebrews 5:12-6:1). The Bible is not a vending machine—it is a banquet.

Having a hard time naming your new pup?
Go online and you'll find plenty of websites
that will help you out. You can choose
a name for your dog from any number
of languages, including Latin.

PAMELA McQUADE

Sometimes the heart sees
what is invisible to the eye.

H. JACKSON BROWN JR.

Thanks, Lord!

- -

Thank You, Lord, for giving me a
dog who reminds me of the joy in life.
When people depress me with bad
news, my dog points out that there's
still reason to remain cheerful:
We still have each other and
a good game of ball.

A Strong Finish

Blessed is the one who perseveres under trial because, having stood the test, that person will receive the crown of life that the Lord has promised to those who love him.

JAMES 1:12 NIV

When Beverly adopted a six-month-old cocker spaniel named Princess, she decided to enroll her in obedience school. The feisty pup had several bad habits—chewing up shoes, shredding toilet paper, and barking at the neighbors. Worst of all, she refused to come when summoned. This was especially problematic when Princess wriggled out of her collar on walks. She would take off running across the neighborhood, ignoring Beverly's calls. But surely obedience training would take care of all of that, right?

With great excitement, Beverly showed up at the first class, ready to get to work. The trainer was patient and kind, and encouraged all of the dog owners to be the same. The first week, they were led through a couple of simple exercises: sit and stay. Unfortunately, Princess ran around the room, completely ignoring her master's commands. The trainer assured Beverly this would get better, if she would just keep working at it. Unfortunately the second week wasn't much better than the first.

By the third week, Princess was the only dog in class who refused to cooperate. Beverly grimaced as the other dog owners showed off the tricks their loveable pooches had conquered. After a while, Beverly began to ask herself, "Why did I even pay for this class? I'm certainly not getting my money's worth." Before long, she and Princess simply dropped out of obedience school. What was the point, anyway?

Sometimes we're like Beverly, aren't we? We set off to accomplish a task that the Lord has given us to do, determined we'll see it through to the end. Our obedience is unquestionable. Then things get hard. . .or don't go as we planned. Before long, we're frustrated, wondering why we ever signed on to do it in the first place. Our determination wavers, and our desire to finish well goes right out the window. Eventually, we just give up.

The Bible teaches that we should persevere, keep on keeping on. God doesn't want us to give up, especially when things get tough. That's the time to dig deep and recommit yourself to a strong finish.

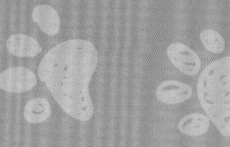

"Let a sleeping dog lie."
It is a poor old maxim,
and nothing in it: Anybody
can do it, you don't have
to employ a dog.
MARK TWAIN

Clearly, dogs believe every day should
include at least one treat, whether it's a
long walk in the park or a tasty bone.
They know how to appreciate the
simple but good things in life.
PAMELA MCQUADE

Fur Count

Lord, thank You for the deep
dog–human bond. May people who
have lost their beloved companions
be comforted by Your deep love
and know that not one bit of
fur was uncounted by You.

Open Your Ears

Not one of you has ever given ear to His [God's] voice or
seen His form (His face—what He is like). [You have always
been deaf to His voice and blind to the vision of Him.]

JOHN 5:37 AMP

Our springer spaniels, Max and Ginger, both went deaf in their old
age. Fortunately, we could still communicate with them. First we would
clap our hands to get their attention. Once their eyes were on us, we
used hand signals for commands to stay, come, sit, and shake.

Sometimes we ourselves are deaf when it comes to God's voice. We
allow our ears to be filled with the clamor of the world. During those
times, God sometimes makes a loud noise to get our attention. At Jesus'
baptism, God's voice boomed, telling the world Jesus was His beloved
Son. But even after that miraculous message, people still did not hear.
For the apostle Paul, God went to extremes with not only a mighty
voice but a blinding flash from heaven.

If you haven't heard God's voice lately, try tuning out the world
long enough to give Him your total and complete attention. Allow
"deaf" to take a holiday by opening your ears to His Word.

No day is so bad it can't be fixed with a nap.

CARRIE SNOW

Noticed it on a snowy day? The grown-ups
are all going about with long faces,
but look at the children—and the dogs?
They know what snow's made for.

C. S. Lewis

What is more agreeable than one's home?

Marcus Tullius Cicero

Go with the Flow

Lord, I know my dog was bred for
a certain purpose, and I can't change
those inbred traits, no matter how hard
I try. Help me to accept those things
I can't change, develop his good
points, and love him no matter what.

Beyond Our Sin

And God is faithful; he will not let you be
tempted beyond what you can bear.
But when you are tempted, he will also
provide a way out so that you can endure it.

1 CORINTHIANS 10:13 NIV

By all accounts, Copper was a well-behaved miniature dachshund. One day Copper's owner, Katie, left him alone in the house for a couple of hours while she went shopping. He decided a little investigation was in order and quickly discovered a jar of Vaseline on her bedside table. It didn't take much effort to get that jar down and pry the top off. The contents inside were slippery, but tasty, at least the first few licks. After consuming about half of the jar he gave up, deciding he'd had enough.

By the time his owner arrived home, Copper was feeling a little queasy. More than a little, actually. Katie searched high and low for her pup but couldn't find him. Copper—one sick little guy—was hiding under the bed. She eventually found him there, along with the half-eaten jar of Vaseline. It took a little prying, but Katie managed to coax Copper out into the open. He came with tail tucked in and head hanging low, knowing he would be scolded. Thankfully, this was one of those cases where Katie felt he'd learned a tough enough lesson already.

After a bit of research on the World Wide Web, Katie realized this situation would probably resolve itself without a trip to the vet's office. Oh, but what a terrible night Copper had. That self-inflicted oil and lube job did quite a number on his tummy. Copper paid a heavy price for succumbing to temptation.

We're a lot like Copper when it comes to sin, aren't we? We see something just beyond our reach, and it's oh, so tempting! With a little extra effort, we manage to snag it and take our first bite, convinced it's going to be wonderful. Eventually, however, reality hits. We realize that we've risked everything for something that can actually bring us harm.

Shame overwhelms us at this point, and we hide away in the shadows of darkness, hoping no one will find us. And when our owner—the Lord—coaxes us into His presence, we come with head hanging low. But He welcomes us anyway, convinced we have learned the appropriate lesson from our actions.

In the end, sin is never pretty. In some cases, the consequences are downright ugly. But we serve a God who sees beyond our sin and offers grace and forgiveness when we ask. All He asks is that we come out from under the bed and own up to what we've done.

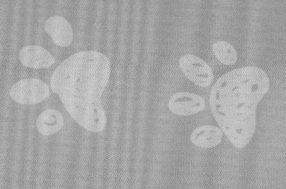

Why do dachshunds wear
their ears inside out?
P. G. WODEHOUSE

Bulldogs are adorable,
with faces like toads that
have been sat on.
COLETTE

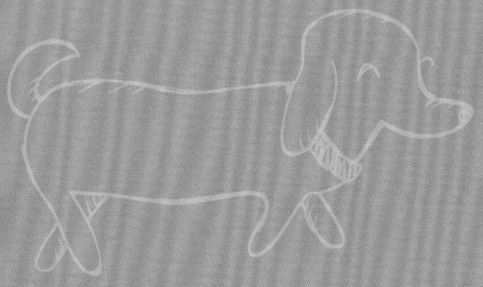

Home and Love

Lord, I often hear about dogs
who don't have homes. Help me
do my part to help those homeless
companions find the people
who will love them.

Precious Quarry

> Now the Berean Jews were of more noble character than those in Thessalonica, for they received the message with great eagerness and examined the Scriptures every day to see if what Paul said was true.
>
> ACTS 17:11 NIV

When I was a child, our family had two English springer spaniels. The first one we named Ginger. When she got too old to retrieve game during a hunt, my father bought a puppy we called Max. Once these dogs got the scent of a squirrel, rabbit, or pheasant, off they'd go, following the trail of their quarry. Although they were both terrific and eager trackers, Max turned out to be gun-shy, making him useless on my father's hunting expeditions and a quivering mass of jelly during thunderstorms or fireworks.

Just like a good hunting dog eagerly searches for his master's game, so should we be panting for God's Word, expectantly looking for His message to us, His willing servants. Would that we would not be Word-shy, but fearless followers, anxious to please Him by seeking out His truths, grasping them in our hearts, courageously applying them to our lives, and reveling with joy because we have found and retrieved precious quarry.

Children left unattended
will be given a puppy or kitten.

ANIMAL SHELTER SIGN

From the lowly perspective of a dog's eyes,
everyone looks short.
PROVERB

A Rescuer's Prayer

Lord, I wish I could wrap my arms
around every dog that needs a home.
Help me rescue every dog I can and to
remember that You hold them all fast,
because they all come from Your arms.

Our Refuge

Start children off on the way they should go,
and even when they are old they will not turn from it.

PROVERBS 22:6 NIV

Puppies love laps. Right after we brought Symba, our collie puppy, into our home, we had to make three trips between our house in Toledo, Ohio, and Johnson City, Tennessee. It's about an eleven-hour drive, and my wife couldn't stand the thought of keeping the new puppy anywhere but on her lap. We were afraid we might be spoiling him for future car trips, but that's the way he wanted to travel. So off we went, me driving and Rob with little Symba on her lap.

It was six months or more after all of this before we had occasion to take him in the car again. My wife opened the back door, meaning for me to help Symba get in the backseat. Then she got in the front passenger seat, and—*wham!*—up jumped Symba who landed on her lap, ready to go!

Only this time his front paws were on the driver's seat and his back legs were hanging out the car door! He had a look on his face that said, "Hey gang, this is cool! Let's go!" After Rob and I stopped laughing ourselves silly and Symba's expression had changed to "Yo, what's the problem here?" we gently eased him back out the door and encouraged him into the backseat, which puzzled him.

But only for a moment. After trying to crawl forward between the front seats and onto Rob's lap one last time, he kindly agreed to take up his new space on the backseat. He has been a perfect traveling dog ever since: quiet, sleepy, happy to be with his family. He doesn't even get yappy when he sees people or other dogs outside that he wants to meet. He's as contented back there as when he was on our laps on those trips to and from Tennessee.

An old adage that reflects scripture says, "As the twig is bent, so grows the tree." Although we thought we might be spoiling Symba, that it might be difficult to retrain him to travel without being on our laps, he was, in fact, learning that traveling in a car is a time of peace, a refuge of sorts. He has us within paw's reach, and we, being belted into our car seats, are a captive audience. Our presence makes the car a refuge to him, as God is to us. And that's peace to him, as it is to us. "The righteous will rejoice in the Lord and take refuge in him" (Psalm 64:10 NIV).

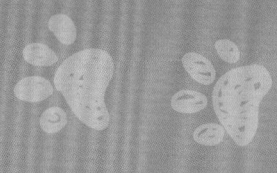

Any member introducing a dog into the
Society's premises shall be liable to
a fine of one pound. Any animal leading
a blind person shall be deemed to be a cat.
RULE 46, OXFORD UNION SOCIETY, LONDON

Anybody who doesn't know
what soap tastes like never washed a dog.
FRANKLIN P. JONES

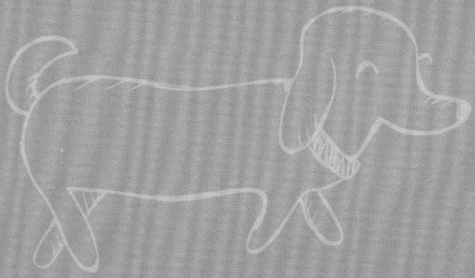

"Just a Dog"

Lord, to many people I know this
is "just a dog." But she is Your creation,
designed with a sensitive nose, fast legs,
and a wide-open heart. Thank You for
this special gift You've given me.
May she never be "just a dog" to me.

Old-Fashioned Comeuppance

"Don't pick on people, jump on their failures,
criticize their faults—unless, of course, you want the same
treatment. That critical spirit has a way of boomeranging.
It's easy to see a smudge on your neighbor's face
and be oblivious to the ugly sneer on your own."

MATTHEW 7:1-3 MSG

Amy's dog, Cooper, loves to wander about the neighborhood. Not all the neighbors appreciate Cooper's wanderlust. So to keep the big dog in his own yard—and still give him some freedom—Amy had an electric fence installed. Cooper's electrified collar serves the duo well. Amy knows Cooper will stay where he belongs. Cooper knows a price is to be paid for breaking the rules and going through the invisible fence: an unpleasant zap! The arrangement works for both of them and all the neighbors—most of the time.

One day the collar couldn't keep Cooper corralled. Cooper saw something too inviting to ignore. He decided a little pain was worth the gain. Gritting his teeth, Cooper bolted through the invisible fence. The zap didn't slow him down; he was off and running!

When Amy saw that Cooper had fled the premises, she had to go hunt down her dog. She finally found him and led him back home.

Cooper came home alongside Amy, his tail between his legs. When they reached their house, Cooper sat his doggie derriere down and wouldn't budge.

No way was he going to get zapped twice! Getting out was one thing—getting back in was something else again. It wasn't worth it. He whined and resisted, easily outweighing Amy. Cooper well remembered his departing jolt. He wasn't about to get another to get back in. Amy finally realized why Cooper wouldn't move.

"Oh! Sorry about that, buddy." She removed his collar, and Cooper immediately went into the yard. Unfortunately for Amy, she followed Cooper into their yard, forgetting what she held in her hand.

Zzzzzzzzzzzap!

Amy looked at Cooper. Was that the slightest suggestion of a smirk she saw on his muzzle?

How often do we wish secretly for other people to "get what's coming to them"? Whether it's a rude driver cutting us off in traffic or a coworker whose sloppy work makes our job tougher, we're quick to wish for old-fashioned comeuppance to come down on their heads. From the Old Testament through the New, we're warned about wanting others to get what they deserve—but not us.

In the New Testament, our warning rings loud and clear: 'With the measure you use, it will be measured to you—and even more' (Mark 4:24 NIV). Before we point a finger at someone else, we need to consider the remaining three that point back at us. God makes the rules and the judgment calls. Just like Cooper's collar, His rules work the same for all of us.

Recollect that the Almighty, who gave
the dog to be companion of our pleasures
and our toils, hath invested him with a
nature noble and incapable of deceit.

Sir Walter Scott

Although the dispositions of dogs
are as various as their forms. . .to the credit
of their name be it said, a dog never
sullies his mouth with an untruth.

Alfred Elwes

Homeless Pups

When I see an ad showing a hurting pup, my heart reaches out, Lord. I understand why some people end up taking in more animals than they can care for. But help me to be wise in caring, however many dogs I own.

Firmly Footed

Apply your heart to instruction,
and your ears to words of knowledge.
PROVERBS 23:12 NKJV

Willie was the cutest puggle in the neighborhood. He lived in an apartment in the suburbs with his owner, Todd. Todd was a graphic artist and was gone for long periods of time during the day. Todd had recently met Willie at the Denver Dumb Friends Rescue Mission. It was love at first sight for both of them. Willie put on quite a show for Todd, hoping, of course, to impress with nuzzling and whining. The decision was an easy one for Todd when Willie placed his right front paw on Todd's hand as he knelt before him.

Through the first few weeks, the two of them grew more and more secure in each other's love and trust, so Willie was adapting to spending time alone waiting for his owner to come home at night. Todd was teaching Willie to fetch, sit, roll over, and speak. Willie didn't mind performing as long as it meant a walk in the park or a doggie treat afterward. He was quite the showman when necessary.

There was one little problem, however, that Todd was not able to resolve with any training or bribery. Willie loved shoes. Not to wear. He loved to eat them. He loved them for breakfast, for lunch, for a snack, and any other time he felt hungry. He even loved to eat them when he didn't feel hungry.

As one can imagine, this was not something Todd was willing to accept. Todd had replaced multiple pairs of shoes, and his patience was wearing thin with Willie's behavior. He knew he had to put his foot down!

Early one Saturday morning Todd awakened, made coffee, and dressed for a morning jog. Willie already recognized Todd's weekend routine and readied himself by grabbing the leash and running to the front door. Willie ran adjacent to Todd, carefree and footloose, enjoying the cool morning air. It wasn't until they reached the fork in the path that Willie became aware of a change in their route. Todd led them to the right and continued down the path on the way downtown.

Shortly they reached the doorway of the North Denver Goodwill store. Todd opened the door and led Willie through the store toward the shoe department. There they found hundreds of pairs of used shoes. All rather odiferous, ragged, and homey. Todd escorted Willie slowly through each row, shoe after shoe after shoe.

Willie sniffed and snuffled and sniffed and snuffled until Todd was sure he wanted to get out of that store! Still Todd continued to lead Willie among the shoes, not intending to miss even one pair. Willie winced and whined, and finally, they started for the door. Todd smiled as he walked outside then knelt beside Willie. Willie had learned a lesson about greed and obedience that day. Todd had done this solely for Willie's own good. From that day forth, the relationship of dog and owner was firmly footed.

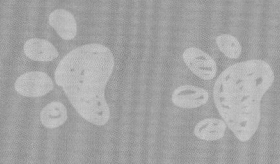

The reason dogs have so many
friends is because they wag
their tails instead of their tongues.

UNKNOWN

If animals could speak, the dog would
be a blundering outspoken fellow;
but the cat would have the rare
grace of never saying a word too much.

MARK TWAIN

Friendship

- -

Though my dog is my best friend, Lord, may
he never be my only friend. Help me to build
relationships with other dog lovers, in the dog park,
on walks, and by sharing the joys of having
a dog with others.

Welcome Home

"So he got up and went to his father. But while
he was still a long way off, his father saw him and
was filled with compassion for him; he ran to his son,
threw his arms around him and kissed him."

Luke 15:20 NIV

Molly, a miniature schnauzer, was an indoor dog. Oh, she got to play in the backyard, too; but her world, as she knew it, was the inside of the house. She had every square inch memorized. Because it was so familiar, she often felt a little bored. She wondered if she might be missing out on something bigger, grander.

Oftentimes Molly would watch as Gillian, her owner, would open the front door and head off to some unknown place. That door began to represent freedom to Molly. She made a vow that one day she would go through it and explore the world on the other side.

Sure enough, the following week she spied an opportunity. Just as Gillian came in, Molly shot out. . .fast as you please! Once outside, she marveled at what she saw! Houses, cars, and people abounded. She began to run, run, run, more excited than ever. Oh, the possibilities! Off in the distance, she heard her master's voice calling, but Molly refused to turn around. Not now! Not when she was having such a blast!

Before long, she was on the sidewalk, chasing a boy with a ball.

The fun continued as Molly saw a pile of leaves. She jumped in them, and they scattered. The wind picked up several of them and blew them into the street. Molly ran after them, determined to catch one in her teeth. Oh, what fun!

Suddenly, she heard a terrible noise. The squeal of tires! A honking horn! Seconds later, a car loomed over her. Yikes! She'd almost been hit. Molly rushed to the side of the road, panting. The man in the car got out and started hollering at her. Then, as her master came running, the man yelled at her, too. Molly couldn't stop shaking.

A wave of relief washed over her as Gillian reached down and scooped her into her arms, speaking words of love over her. The mean man in the car took off, and they were left alone. Molly gave Gillian a hundred kisses on her cheeks and promised never to run off again.

Have you ever felt like Molly? Maybe you've walked with God for years and lived an obedient life. But, like that curious puppy, you wondered what was on the other side of the door. Perhaps the desire to "explore" became too strong, so you wandered away, finding many adventures and exciting things to do. Things that seemed harmless.

And then. . .the squeal of tires. Honking horns. You stumbled into a situation that put your life—physically or symbolically speaking—in danger. Suddenly, things were spiraling out of control. Everything—and everyone—turned against you.

Oh, the joy of knowing the Father waits with arms extended for you to turn back to Him! He longs for you to come back to the safety of His embrace. Today, relish the love of your heavenly Father as He welcomes you back home.

Dogs do speak, but only to those
who know how to listen.
ORHAN PAMUK

Wild dogs sleep in dens, and their
domestic counterparts also favor a sheltered
sleeping spot that feels like a den—hence
the under-the-bed or under-the-table
sleeping habits of many domestic dogs.
PAMELA MCQUADE

Beware of the man who does not talk,
and the dog that does not bark.
CHEYENNE PROVERB

Forgiveness

Lord, my dog may not be perfect,
but I still love her. Help me to encourage
her and focus on the things she does
right. Remind me, as anger threatens,
that when I fail, You still love me.

Free and Clean

Let us throw off everything that hinders and the sin
that so easily entangles. And let us run with perseverance
the race marked out for us, fixing our eyes on Jesus,
the pioneer and perfecter of faith.

HEBREWS 12:1-2 NIV

It all began when he was a puppy. Kendall's German shorthair, Lucky, developed an attachment to a teddy bear. In the house, Lucky carries Teddy around from room to room unless something else has his undivided attention. Even though Teddy is roughly the same size as Lucky, Lucky holds on to the stuffed bear with the tenacity of a pit bull. Lucky must follow only one rule: the teddy bear stays in the house. He isn't allowed to drag his bedtime buddy out in the dirt.

That's why Kendall was puzzled one day when she saw Lucky carting his teddy bear around the yard—or what she thought was his teddy bear. To Kendall's horror, the brown furry thing Lucky had in his paws wasn't his teddy bear. Lucky had killed a groundhog. He wasn't about to part with the dead baggage. He was cuddling up to his quarry just like he did to Teddy. Gagging and grumbling, Kendall managed to get Lucky away from the groundhog so she could clean up Lucky. She left the uglier deed—the burial of Teddy's dead twin, the groundhog—to her husband.

Not much time passed. Again Kendall noticed that Lucky wasn't running around the yard much. It couldn't be, could it? Ugh! Not again!

Lucky had dug up the dead groundhog and was carting it around the yard. Now the mess was worse. Lucky was snuggling up with the dirtied, bloodied, dried-up, dog-drool-covered, deceased groundhog. Kendall nearly lost it—again.

For round two, she gave Not-So-Lucky his second bath of the day— not to mention a second shower for herself. Kendall's husband took care to dig a deeper hole outside their yard, for what they hoped would be the groundhog's final resting place. They both breathed a sigh of relief when the second "planting" worked.

We don't have to carry around, or be weighted down by, the dead deeds of our past. Our own consciences—or even other people—can dig up our past sins and load us down with guilt. But if we have received Christ and trust in Him, we've been released from sin's hold on us (see Romans 8:1–2). Jesus forgives us. He frees us from the baggage of our past. We don't need to dig it up.

Jesus dealt with our sin at the cross. The Lord has separated us from the dead deeds of our past, just as Kendall separated Lucky from the unfortunate groundhog. And as Lucky was clean after his super scrubbing, so has our Savior thoroughly washed us up and readied us to go on.

With the dead groundhog finally laid to rest, Lucky stayed free— and clean—of his groundhog baggage. Thanks to the Lord Jesus, and with all of heaven cheering us on (see Hebrews 12:1), we're clean and baggage-free, too!

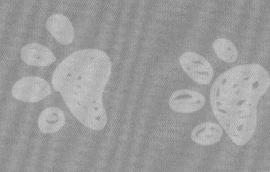

A good hound never barks
on a cold trail.

THORNTON W. BURGESS

Think of your dog as a sponge,
willing to take everything in and
eager to learn new things. . . . A dog is
a living creature with a hungry mind
and a great capacity for love
and gratitude—as long as you keep
her interested and excited about life.

TAMAR GELLER

For I am persuaded beyond doubt (am sure)
that neither death nor life, nor angels nor principalities,
nor things impending and threatening nor things to come,
nor powers, nor height nor depth, nor anything else
in all creation will be able to separate us from the
love of God which is in Christ Jesus our Lord.

ROMANS 8:38–39 AMP

"Understand, therefore, that the LORD your God is
indeed God. He is the faithful God who keeps his covenant
for a thousand generations and lavishes his unfailing love
on those who love him and obey his commands."

DEUTERONOMY 7:9 NLT

A Small Price to Pay

A happy heart is good medicine and a cheerful
mind works healing, but a broken spirit dries up the bones.

PROVERBS 17:22 AMP

Our loving shepherd-Lab, Zoey, has a servant's heart. That's what I told myself every time I'd load the dishwasher and she was immediately there, licking rinsed silverware right onto the floor. It was annoying, but if I reminded myself that she thought she was helping, it didn't bother me as much.

One evening like any other, I was loading the dishes while two of my sons, Mitch and Wes, were in the kitchen, making a sandwich and reading mail, respectively. While the boys and I chatted about the events of the day, Zoey was at her post by my side, head poised over the sliding bottom basket that was pulled out and getting filled with dishes, pans, and silverware. She rested her neck on the edge of the sturdy sliding basket, leaned slightly inward, straining for more drips of water, and suddenly she panicked beyond reason.

The moment I realized that her collar was caught on the basket was the same nanosecond the kitchen seemed to explode in one fluid motion. The crashing noise hit my senses before the flash of flying dishes, glass, and metal, followed by Zoey attached to a large dish basket with small wheels, followed by a portable island on big wheels getting pulled into the melee, pitching forward with its shelves of breakable contents looking to be a part of the excitement.

We stood there stunned for half a second before I yelled to Mitch, closest to the dog, "Grab Zoey!" who was still in motion. Wes simultaneously caught the island on wheels before it crashed over. Zoey broke free from the heavy metal basket, which she probably thought had attacked her, and she fled the scene in fear.

"What just happened?" Wes said, more as a statement than a question.

His youngest brother, Dexter, running in to see what all the commotion was about, found us all standing still, surrounded by shards of glass, forks, knives, bowls, and the second broken Corelle dish in fifteen years. Let me tell you—when they break, they really break; we're talking jagged daggers. But no one was hurt.

We all just started laughing hysterically. Zoey peeked around the corner as if asking if the attack basket had left yet. "Is it safe to return?" her eyes asked. We worked together to clear paths for each other, laughing all along as we slowly cleaned up the unusual mess and retold the story to Dexter and then Dad when he got home, then later on the phone to the oldest brother, Trevor, away at college. Laughing again.

I later thought how grateful I am that we found the humor in that, instead of the inconvenience. How a few broken dishes are a small price to pay to find happy hearts in one of the many messes of life. We've laughed many times since. Zoey, however, prefers now to drink her water out of the same old bowl, or the cat's bowl, but that's another story.

My near little, queer little, dear little dog,
So fearless of man, yet afraid of a frog!
The nearest and queerest and dearest of all
The race that is loving and winning and small;
The sweetest, most faithful, the truest and best
Dispenser of merriment, love and unrest!

COLETTA RYAN

One dog barks at something,
the rest bark at him.

CHINESE PROVERB

Appreciation

- -

Lord, I give my dog a simple dog treat
and he acts as if he's received a five-course
dinner. May I be that appreciative of the
ordinary, good things You give me.

From the Inside Out

"And why worry about a speck in your
friend's eye when you have a log in your own?"

LUKE 6:41 NLT

Angel was a two-year-old Chihuahua with a bit of an attitude problem. She had a tendency to snap at people, and usually when they least expected it. Fortunately. . .or unfortunately. . .Angel belonged to Donna, a woman who let her get away with anything and everything. Talk about spoiled! If Angel made a mess, Donna cleaned it up without scolding. If the dog snapped at the neighbors, Donna made excuses.

Despite her mean-spirited nature, Angel was often dressed in adorable little doggie outfits and sparkling collars. Donna particularly loved putting her pup in a precious angel costume. Others saw the irony but not Donna. Oh no. She would take the ornery pup into public to show off the costume. Folks passing by would see her and ooh and ahh. Many would make the mistake of reaching out to pet her as they carried on about how darling she was. They learned very quickly that Angel was no angel. A little demon was more like it. Unfortunately, a couple of folks learned this too late, after she snapped at them.

After an episode where Angel bit a neighbor, Donna finally realized the error of her ways and signed the naughty pup up for obedience training. Though it took a considerable amount of work, the little beast was finally tamed. Before long her inside matched her outside. She could wear that angel costume. . .and mean it.

Sometimes people are a lot like Angel. . .all dolled up on the outside, putting forth a near-perfect image. They want others to see only the good and not the bad. However, their true colors shine through when you bump up against them. This is even true of church folks. (Gasp!) Sometimes believers work extra hard to put forth a good image, concerned about how they are viewed by others. Then something happens and they get riled up. . .and watch out! The inside doesn't match the outside anymore!

So, where do you stand? Are you really who you say you are, who you present yourself to be? Or have you—especially among your Christian peers—started to put on a front because you're afraid to let people see the real you? Are you worried they won't like what they see if you let your guard down or stop pretending?

It's time to get honest. Real. If you're struggling with an internal problem like anger or jealousy, allow the Lord to heal you from the inside out. Let Him peel back the facade and do a true, intimate work. He longs to see you healed and whole. And look on the bright side— once His work is done, you won't have to plaster on a smile. The joy will bubble up naturally! Talk about being dressed from the inside out!

Dogs howl to "talk" to other members
of the pack. Generally speaking, a howl says
"Where are you?" If your dog howls
when left alone, it is bored.

BRUCE FOGLE

The dog is the most faithful of animals
and would be much esteemed were it not
so common. Our Lord God has made
His greatest gift the commonest.

MARTIN LUTHER

That is what the Scriptures mean when they say,
"No eye has seen, no ear has heard, and no mind has
imagined what God has prepared for those who love him."
1 CORINTHIANS 2:9 NLT

And hope does not put us to shame, because
God's love has been poured out into our hearts
through the Holy Spirit, who has been given to us.
ROMANS 5:5 NIV

We have confidence in the Lord that you are doing and will
continue to do the things we command. May the Lord direct
your hearts into God's love and Christ's perseverance.
2 THESSALONIANS 3:4–5 NIV

Our True Selves

For if anyone only listens to the Word without
obeying it and being a doer of it, he is like a man
who looks carefully at his [own] natural face in a mirror;
for he thoughtfully observes himself, and then goes
off and promptly forgets what he was like.

JAMES 1:23–24 AMP

As a puppy, Durham had an amazingly elusive nemesis. He was
only seen when Durham stood in front of our stove and gazed into
its window. That's because Durham's rival was his own reflection! He
panted when Durham panted, whined when he whined, and barked
when he barked. What a strange creature! And how frustrating for
Durham that he could never reach him!

Fortunately, we humans are a bit smarter than dogs. We know that
the face we see in the mirror (or stove window) is actually our own. But
are we seeing a soon-to-be-forgotten reflection or our true selves in
the light of God's Word?

James advises us to look carefully at scripture and then study
ourselves, content not just with hearing how we are to be conformed
to Christ's image but actually making the changes and improvements
God wants us to make—without whining or barking. That's something
to reflect on.

Leaping, loping, four abreast, they
came plunging like so many North Winds
to their party! Streak of Snow—Glow of Fire—
Frozen Mud—Sun-Spot!—Yelping-mouthed—
Slapping-tailed! Backs bristling! Legs stiffening!
Wolf Hound, Setter, Bull Dog, Dalmatian—each
according to his kind, hurtling, crowding!

ELEANOR HALLOWELL ABBOTT

I like a bit of a mongrel myself,
whether it's a man or a dog.
They're the best for everyday.

GEORGE BERNARD SHAW

153

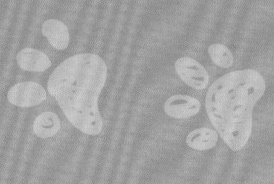

Stewardship

Lord, You've given me this dog to care for. Help me share the loving-kindness I've received from You. Remind me, when I'm tired and cranky, that I'm accountable to You for my care for him.

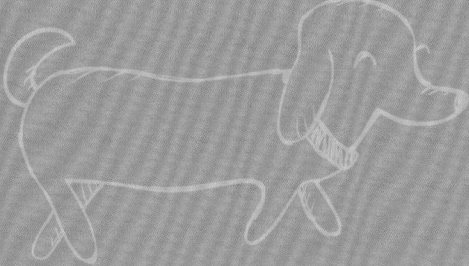

Boldness

So that we may boldly say, The Lord is my helper,
and I will not fear what man shall do unto me.

HEBREWS 13:6 KJV

Some dogs are bolder by nature than others, and some love to yap more than others. Such was the case with Sasha, a thirteen-pound red doxie (aka, dachshund). A city dog at heart, she hardly knew what to do with herself when her owner, Annie, took her to the country for a couple of days. Suddenly the entire landscape of her existence changed. Instead of concrete sidewalks, postage-stamp lawns, and suburban houses, Sasha was introduced to wide-open fields, barns, and tractors. The most interesting thing of all? The tall four-legged creatures in the pasture. Horses.

When Sasha heard them whinnying, she felt sure they were set to attack. The bold doxie flew into action to protect her owner from these strange, elusive creatures. Now, she'd never been introduced to a horse before, but the sheer size of the magnificent beasts didn't scare her. . .not from a distance, anyway. No sir. She ran full steam ahead, yapping all the way. Her plan? To bite them in the ankles. To protect her owner from harm!

Only one problem. The closer she got to them, the bigger they appeared! And, as Sasha drew near, the horse in the front began to take several rapid steps toward her. Yikes! She had never planned on a counterattack! Fear took hold, and she stopped in her tracks. It was one thing to run after him; another altogether to have him run after her!

Have you walked a mile in Sasha's paws? Can you relate? Sometimes life presents us with extreme obstacles and we run boldly toward them, ready to conquer them head-on. Fear never enters into it. Pure adrenaline drives us forward. Then, as we get closer, we begin to feel threatened. Our boldness slips away. We cower in fear.

Today, the Lord wants to remind you that no matter how big your problem might be, He is bigger still. No matter how tall the mountain, He can move it. Even the most "magnificent beast" is tiny in His sight. So, don't let the enemy call your bluff. Don't back down. Instead, run with confidence, knowing the Lord is right there with you, giving you the boldness you need to see things through.

Whoever loveth me, loveth my hound.

THOMAS MORE

It's nice to have a pet that offers unconditional love,
someone who doesn't talk back. I love cats, but cats
take you on their terms. My golden retriever could have
a broken leg, and his teeth could be falling out, but if
I walk in the door, he'll wag his tail until it hurts.

BOB VETERE

We long for an affection altogether ignorant
of our faults. Heaven has accorded this to
us in the uncritical canine attachment.

GEORGE ELIOT

*Pay attention to advice
and accept correction,
so you can live sensibly.*

PROVERBS 19:20 CEV

Everything God says is true—and it's a
shield for all who come to him for safety.

PROVERBS 30:5 CEV

I have written to you who are God's children because
you know the Father. I have written to you who are mature
in the faith because you know Christ, who existed from the
beginning. I have written to you who are young in the faith
because you are strong. God's word lives in your hearts,
and you have won your battle with the evil one.

1 JOHN 2:14 NLT

Eyes on Jesus

Pattern yourselves after me
[follow my example], as I imitate
and follow Christ (the Messiah).

1 CORINTHIANS 11:1 AMP

When Max joined our family, Ginger was not happy with the new kid on her block. But she did find a way to tolerate him. Eager to please, Max followed Ginger everywhere and imitated everything she did. That included squatting to relieve himself instead of lifting his leg like others of his gender. Max's problem was that there was no male dog in his realm from which he could learn boy dog behavior.

As Christians, we are called to pattern our lives after Christ. But sometimes we, too, deviate from the example that God has set before us and end up imitating the sinful instead of the Savior. That's because when our eyes are on the temporal instead of the spiritual, we wind up on the wrong path, looking to please people instead of God.

To stay in focus and on the right road, keep your eyes on Jesus. Following His example, you'll find true relief.

Always remember to forget
the things that made you sad.
But never forget to remember
the things that made you glad.
Always remember to forget
the friends that proved untrue.
But never forget to remember
those who have stuck by you.

IRISH BLESSING

The motion of [a dog's tail] is full of
meaning. There is the slow wag of anger;
the gentle wag of contentment; the brisker
wag of joy: and what can be more
mutely expressive than the limp
states of sorrow, humility, and fear?

ALFRED ELWES

Wondrous Design

- -

Lord, You've helped me appreciate
how wondrously You've made the
dog. Out of all the animals You made,
this one was designed as my special
companion and friend. Thank You.

Victorious

Be alert and of sober mind.
Your enemy the devil prowls
around like a roaring lion
looking for someone to devour.

1 PETER 5:8 NIV

Jodi's dog, Max, was a small Yorkshire terrier. Max was a tiny little thing but could be very aggressive when he wanted to be. Max didn't care much for strangers. He didn't like the mailman, and he threw a fit when anyone stuck a pamphlet in the door. And when out-of-town guests came to visit, it took the little dog days to warm up. But Max's mortal enemy was the vacuum cleaner. Max hated the vacuum with a passion and would attack the contraption on sight. Jodi stored the vacuum in the closet and dreaded the weekly cleaning when Max and the vacuum would battle "to the death." Jodi always tried to vacuum the carpets when Max was busy with other things or playing in the backyard with his favorite ball. But as soon as Max would hear the vacuum's hideous voice, he would race inside to protect his home from the ferocious monster.

Max would jump on the vacuum, scratching it and pawing at it through the entire length of the house. He would squeal and yelp, demanding that the beast give up and go back to his hideout. Max always seemed to win the fight. By the time Jodi had finished cleaning the downstairs, Max was hoarse, but the vacuum stopped and went back to wherever it came from. Max felt victorious every time.

One morning during a particularly vicious battle between the dog and his enemy, Jodi remembered that she had left a pot boiling on the stove. Without shutting off the vacuum, she ran to the kitchen to tend to the pot. Max was momentarily distracted, watching his master run off. Not paying attention to what was happening, Max looked around the corner to see what Jodi was doing. He backed right into the vacuum extension, which immediately grabbed his long hair and sucked him in. The vacuum was winning. Max was stuck. He could not get the machine to let go of his hair. He yipped and yelped for help. Jodi heard the struggle and came to Max's rescue. She turned off the vacuum, and Max ran for cover.

First Corinthians 10:12 (NIV) says that "if you think you are standing firm, be careful that you don't fall!" In other words, don't ever think you are so strong that you can't be shaken. You just might get knocked down a few pegs! Just like the vacuum, the devil is always watching and waiting for us to trip up. He wants us to be momentarily distracted so he can swoop in and catch us off guard. But if we keep our eyes on Jesus at all times, the devil doesn't stand a chance.

A bone to the dog is not charity. Charity
is the bone shared with the dog, when you
are just as hungry as the dog.

JACK LONDON

A dog has one aim in life. . .to bestow his heart.

J. R. ACKERLEY

He loves us not only in his
consciousness and his intelligence:
the very instinct of his race,
the entire unconsciousness of his
species, it appears, think only of us,
dream only of being useful to us.

MAURICE MAETERLINCK

Your word is a lamp for my feet,
a light on my path.
PSALM 119:105 NIV

Let the teaching of Christ live in you richly.
Use all wisdom to teach and instruct
each other by singing psalms, hymns,
and spiritual songs with thankfulness
in your hearts to God.
COLOSSIANS 3:16 NCV

Our Hiding Place

You are my hiding place; you will
protect me from trouble and surround
me with songs of deliverance.

PSALM 32:7 NIV

A lot of dogs aren't afraid of anything. Or so it seems. But even though Jake would have protected his master from just about anything, he was afraid of lightning. Anytime there was a storm overhead, Jake would scurry inside and find a safe hiding place. Whenever the thunder rolled and the lightning struck, Jake would cower in fear, whimpering and shivering nervously until the storm was over.

After a long day at work, Jake's master, Sarah, stood by the exit, trying to muster the courage to run out into the rain. She was disappointed when she realized that she had left her umbrella in the car. Shielding her head with a magazine, Sarah hurried to her car and started home. Twenty minutes later, she pulled into the garage and ran into the house to find Jake. She knew he would be scared to death because this storm was unusually strong and loud. Jake wasn't in his usual hiding spot, so Sarah searched the house. He wasn't under the bed, he wasn't in the bathtub, and he wasn't hiding behind the couch. Sarah was getting worried, so she went to the kitchen to grab the phone and call the neighbor. That's when she saw the mess.

Every pot, pan, and storage container she owned was scattered on the kitchen floor. The cookie sheets were under the refrigerator. Her mixer was lying sideways next to her antique cookie jar. Even her old toaster, the one she hadn't seen in years and kept in the back of the cupboard, was lying haphazardly on the floor. Sarah opened the cupboard door where the pots and pans should have been and found Jake. He had removed everything from the cupboard and found a safer hiding place. Sarah chuckled at the dog, helped him out of the cupboard, and held him on the kitchen floor until the storm subsided.

God's Word tells us that "perfect love drives out fear" (1 John 4:18 NIV). When Sarah opened the cupboard and held her dog during the storm, his fear went away. His master was loving him and protecting him. We all have so many fears. Some are even paralyzing. Our heavenly Father wants to be our hiding place. No matter what you are facing, His arms are open wide, and He is always willing to hold you during the storm.

"I'll be good, really!" plead the rescue dog's eyes. You take him home, shower him with affection, train him in your ways. In time, he finally feels loved. One day he empties the trash can on your floor, breaks into the dog treats, and chews six rolls of toilet paper. Congratulations, you've bonded!

PAMELA McQUADE

[Being a parent] is tough. If you just want a wonderful little creature to love, you can get a puppy.

BARBARA WALTERS

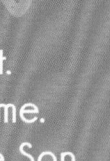

My old self has been crucified with Christ.
It is no longer I who live, but Christ lives in me.
So I live in this earthly body by trusting in the Son
of God, who loved me and gave himself for me.

GALATIANS 2:20 NLT

Know, recognize, and understand therefore
this day and turn your [mind and] heart to it that
the Lord is God in the heavens above and
upon the earth beneath; there is no other.

DEUTERONOMY 4:39 AMP

"But will God really dwell on earth? The heavens,
even the highest heaven, cannot contain you.
How much less this temple I have built!"

1 KINGS 8:27 NIV

What's in Your Soul?

A merry heart maketh a cheerful countenance:
but by sorrow of the heart the spirit is broken.

PROVERBS 15:13 KJV

You know that silly grin on most dogs' faces? A good many dogs appear to find life quite entertaining, and why not? They don't have a care in the world. Their meals are served to them in personalized dishes. They have nice warm beds or at least straw-lined doghouses where they spend their time dreaming of chasing cars, tormenting less vicious creatures, or having their bellies rubbed. Ahh, the privileged lives they lead.

Happy the hound, however, is not happy. At least she doesn't appear to be happy. She waddles around with a pathetic look and her face nearly dragging on the ground. Her countenance is evidence that all her efforts are halfhearted at best.

Truthfully there is no way the dog would ever appear to live up to her name. She's a floppy-eared, wrinkly-skinned basset hound—proof that God has a sense of humor obvious even in His creation. Every pet lover has preferences as to what type of animal they keep, and I suppose it's good for all the "Happys" out there that someone loves them. They just always look so sad. You might think they carried the weight of the world on their shoulders.

Typically when a person approaches a dog, he can determine pretty quickly how the dog feels about his presence. There's the telltale wag of the tail and excited pant that says the dog was just waiting for someone to welcome. On the other hand, some dogs will greet you with a snarl and a snap of the jaws that lets you know you are quite possibly overstepping your bounds.

If Happy is feeling particularly energetic, she might meander up to you out of mere curiosity rather than any real care about your existence. On lazy days she is more likely to observe from a distance. About the only thing that can truly raise her ire is a cat that crosses too closely in her path. Even at that, her expression never changes.

It's easy to feel sorry for the poor thing. She just doesn't seem to fit in. Of course, she doesn't know this, and neither do the other dogs. They get along just fine. They don't worry about her mopey-looking eyes or the fact that we humans want to attribute emotions that might or might not exist. She is what she is; take it or leave it.

So she's a basset hound, and she's supposed to look like that. People are not. The expression on a person's face often tells very much about her. A person with a happy expression is generally more pleasant to be around than someone with a sour look, because what's on your face reflects what's in your soul. Enjoy the humor God has blessed you with. Your friends—and your face—will thank you.

I've caught more ills from people
sneezing over me and giving me virus
infections than from kissing dogs.
Barbara Woodhouse

As much as any animal on earth, dogs express
emotions as purely and clearly as a five-year-old child,
and surely that's part of why we love them so much.
Patricia B. McConnell

Folk will know how large your soul is,
by the way you treat a dog.
Charles F. Doran

My Dog's Needs

- -

Lord, I know You value this dog whom
You've created. May every moment of care I
give to my dog reflect Your love for Your creation,
and may it bring joy to me and my dog.

Eternal Life

Jesus said unto her, I am the resurrection,
and the life: he that believeth in me,
though he were dead, yet shall he live.

JOHN 11:25 KJV

It is said that cats have nine lives. As far as I know, the same has not been said for dogs. One particular Jack Russell, aptly named Russ (because all male Jack Russells on our farm are named Russ—and yes, most of the females are Jackie), seemed to forget for a day that he was, in fact, not feline. Of all the beautiful acres to explore, it appears that those nearest the road are the most attractive. While our farm is lovely, it is not along one of those idyllic little country roads or dirt lanes but smack-dab on the curve of a rather highly, and quickly, traveled road. It is probably not the best playground for small dogs, but they obviously forget the near misses and return for the thrill of adventure or whatever it is that attracts them to such perils.

So on that otherwise beautiful morning, Russ was taking a stroll along the road when around the curve and at a high rate of speed came a car and its mad driver. It took Russ so much by surprise that he had no opportunity to react. Before he knew what was happening, he was lying on the side of the road, still breathing, hanging on to threads of life but all too close to becoming another statistic of involuntary canine-slaughter.

In those same seconds, the car came to a screeching halt, and its badly shaken driver was at Russ's side, willing the little creature to be alive. Soon my husband arrived on the scene. The driver tearfully begged him to allow her to try to nurse Russ back to health. Seeing the hopelessness of the situation, he kindly declined the offer and made Russ as comfortable as possible in the barn. He checked on the little dog from time to time, and Russ continued to pathetically hang on. A few hours later he was gone. Literally. He had disappeared. We figured he had dragged himself off somewhere to die alone, not even giving us a chance to give him a proper burial.

Of course, it wouldn't have been very nice of us to bury him alive, and that was very much the case. He wasn't slowly making his way around or playing the invalid of earlier in the day. Apparently he couldn't stand much of that because the next time we saw him, which was hours after the mishap, he was running around, happy as you please, just like nothing had happened.

That's what happens when a person trusts Christ as Savior. Prior to salvation, we are dead in our sin. We are living a pitiful existence with no hope at all. That's why Christ died and rose again though. He defeated sin, and when we trust Him as Savior, He robs the grave of another victim (see 1 Corinthians 15:55–57). What a wonderful promise of new life. Unlike cats, and maybe Russ, we don't get nine lives. It's important that we give the one we do have to Jesus so that we might have eternal life.

The relationships between man and
dog can often be as complex as that
between man and woman. We have,
own, or are owned by dogs for a great
variety of reasons, not all of them exactly
to our credit. We all want to be loved.

IAN NIALL

Ask of the beasts and they will
teach you the beauty of this earth.

FRANCIS OF ASSISI

Of the animals who live with us, many are
worthy of recognition, and more than all the
others and most faithful to man is the dog.

PLINY THE ELDER

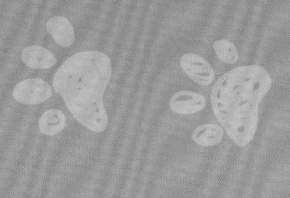

When your words came, I ate them;
they were my joy and my heart's delight,
for I bear your name, LORD God Almighty.

JEREMIAH 15:16 NIV

For the word of God is alive and
powerful. It is sharper than the sharpest
two-edged sword, cutting between soul
and spirit, between joint and marrow.
It exposes our innermost thoughts and desires.

HEBREWS 4:12 NLT